I0149066

Misty Darkness,

A BOOK OF POETRY.

HARKI DHILLON

Copyright © 2014 Harki Dhillon

All rights reserved.

ISBN: 069232657X

ISBN 13: 9780692326572

Library of Congress Control Number: 2014920024

HiCare Inc, Riverside, CA

Index

Some poems from the first book-

Invisible Hands, a book of poetry.

Dedicated to my family
The well from which I drink
My sustenance.

DOLI

Let mine be the last embrace
with my father.
His tears run down my cheek
crying a willing farewell
blessing the way for my life
as my husband, so new, so patient,
so kind
waits to take me into his world.
Let my fathers' anguished gaze
linger forever in my heart
for all his love is there to see.
That moment held my life
from the first cry of my clumsy birth
to this fearless leap
where I will produce a son
who will be the father that I have.

The Crisis

It comes like a storm

not forecast on any wavelength.

It is a fiery wind

it is a deluge

It is wave after wave

breaking

on my crumbling shell of emotions,

the barrier long gone.

Vulnerable.

Visible.

Vanishing.

Unable to hold on

I am consumed.

Enough

Are you in the lagoon
having passed through stormy seas.
Do you feel drained,
with hope a struggling flame
deep within,
to search for happiness,
to search for a kindred soul,
to search for comfort and companionship
and, maybe love.
To shed the cloak of bitterness
with its tendrils
wrapped around each emotional fiber,
to purge regret
and spring to freedom,
to breathe sweet air
without the grip of sadness
the crushing force released,
to remember with courage
the moment you cried
Enough.

The wedding rehearsal

Two years old
ankles and knees
bounce to the rhythm of rap.
Eyes round in wonderment
at adults
in gold and glitter
bouncing to the rhythm of rap.
Grandfather,
smile fixed,
gaze locked
in wonderment
at all his children
bouncing
to the rhythm of rap.
Bride and groom to be,
seek his blessing
as the music fades
replaced by
the joyous notes
of love,
in the hearts
of the bride and groom to be.

Images

As I close my eyes
immersed
in the rhythm of the drums
the eyelids become a screen.
The image
of my daughters
happy and playing,
smiling their innocence,
lifting my heart and
my very being
in lazy elegance
against a turquoise sky.
She, the singer
screams her talent
the drums burst
and
I come back
to the reality
of my body
and my soul.

Dirk

He died of the bloat
that stretched his gleaming coat.
Painful shining eyes
faded away.
The last breath exhaled
as a misty vapor
his soul disappeared into the night.
He had lived with the grace and dignity
of a lord
all animal but definitely human.
Life transferred
by the mystery of the Universe,
all energy and soul
moving so purposefully
to touch man and beast
the same in the west
the same in the east.

When blood turns to water

You fly high on a tapestry of lies
deception in every weave
camouflaged by soaring images
of hope and purity.
You strip the feeble of their fortunes
a blight on the end of their days.
You pillage and rape and plunder
the dreams of generations
with a cold and indifferent smile,
the loot feeding
your debauched life.
Sometimes you come as a stranger
evil incarnate,
sometime, your blood is the same
as you take them to the slaughter.
It is more than evil
when blood turns to water.

The Arrest

The expanse of maroon roofs
congealed
in the heat and glare of the afternoon sun
slowly emerge as distinct homes
bathed in the light
of the evening sun.
The cool clean air
now breaks the lethargy,
people and dogs appear
ambulating aimlessly
in between enthusiastic sprinklers
that proudly exhibit
golden drops of dancing water,
color added
by the bright blue and red lights
of a police cruiser
showing an arrest in progress.
Red back pack
on the thin shoulders
of a young black boy
sitting on his haunches
looking at
the tight brown uniform
on the strong white man
with the big black gun.

The green dress

The bright green dress
defeated
by the gentle slope of the shoulders,
the bright lipstick
hiding poorly
life's worry lines.
The severe black hat
drowning the optimism
that could have been.
If only
your children had not left,
if only
they would hold your hand and smile
and walk in the sunshine
with you
if only
your isolation was not so intense.
You go home to your cat
and your television,
the flickering light
the gentle purring
your consolation and companion

deep into the night,
no last thoughts
before you close your eyes
and drift away.

The folded pages of the past

I fly back
on the wings of memories
to the night with the hunter's moon
and my youth.
The cold wooden stock of the gun
and it's cold metal barrel
rests comfortably in my gloved hands,
mist from my breath
mingles with the mist from the river.
I hear the rustling
of the tall sugarcane,
a menacing contrast
to the silent, subservient wheat field.
The bundled silhouettes
of family and friends
huddled against the cold,
many, now lost
in the folded pages of the past.
A bitterly cold night
brings back a warm fuzzy feeling.
Young as I was then
I felt what it might feel to be a man.

The funeral

A raven cries

a note of anguish,

a myna, her cry of despair.

A pigeon coos,

mourning a lost love.

I am silent and empty,

all feeling

wrenched away into a void,

leaving a void

so deep and so dark.

The cold, forbidding stainless steel doors

open,

reveal the flames,

roaring,

waiting,

competing

with the silent anguish

and the deafening chant

of those left behind.

Belief, faith, love

and looming loneliness

bid a farewell,

which nobody should have to.

The hesitant yet final turn,

away from the now closed doors

stumbling with grief

on numb legs

barely supporting

numb mind and numb body,

helped by a caring,

compassionate circle of family and friends,

providing a crutch

which will have to be discarded

and life will have to go on,

never the same,

never.

The River

The constant swirl
of the gently flowing water,
its depth and color
uniting in its menace,
its changing course
slow and destructive
even as it gives life
to those who pay homage
at its banks,
its constant presence
recording the passage
of history
from the time of its own origin
to its surrender
into the waiting vastness of salinity.
Giving up.

Persecution

My cry is put on a ringtone,

to irritate.

My sleek black coat

and my coal black eyes

are the symbols of evil.

Sorcerers and witches

are my mythical companions.

Shakespeare wrote about me.

Its not really my fault

that Macbeth plunged the dagger

into what's his name.

One of us,

a messenger,

gave bad news to Apollo

who turned our whiteness to black,

forever,

if you in believe that sort of thing.

You were young,

you carried a BB gun

that spat projectiles

which killed us in great numbers,

your only motivation

to prove

you were more clever

as you ambushed us

through half closed doors
when we gathered
for our morning drink
outside your kitchen drain
only to see us fall
yet
we thrive
because we are good.
Does not good always
triumph over evil?
Black is not evil
Black is pure
Black is seductive
Feathers included.

You

Touched your body

so many times

in different ways

in different places.

Touched your soul and

touched your mind

touched your heart

felt alive and exhilarated

felt high

felt low

felt warm

aglow

felt my heartbeat

felt your lips

felt your breath

felt safe

in your embrace.

I hold you

I hold you tight
and the Universe expands
into your being.
I float within you
weightless
chasing an evasive light
in the darkness.
Your tears and sweat
mingle with mine.
Just for a moment
time stands still.

Softly

So softly you hold my world

with a gentle smile,

with a frivolous twirl,

in your loving embrace,

in your hooded gaze.

So softly

we travel the path.

The urn

I look from above
at the reverent hands
that hold the urn,
my physical remains
reduced to ash and bone.
Love and grief and memories
swirl in confusion,
tangible.
They lift the lid,
gently upend the urn
and watch the remains
fall and float and whirl away
into the water.
I hate and fear drowning.
A double death.
So unfair.

My little one

What is in store for you
my little one,
a lifetime ahead of you
and less than half of mine,
maybe.
You are so protected
with the anxiety of love
and the warm embrace of hope
for you to grow and prosper
and learn
and maybe to return the love
you take for granted.
Your first step on your own
a milestone,
the steps
that will take you away from me
even though, now,
you run towards me
with arms outstretched.
You hang onto my leg
with desperation
as you peek at the stranger
a curiosity so intense
that it will take you away one day
to live with a stranger

you make your own.
You listen to stories every night
so you can sleep
with dreams
that make you squirm with delight.
You question and you believe.
How long will that last?
The first pangs of hunger
turns your face
to your mother's breast.
And, after,
you sleep, satisfied,
a simple need, simply given.
These moments,
so intense for me,
none of which you remember,
none of which you can hold dear.
You build your memory bank
of happiness, hoping
the years will compound the interest,
memories that you relate to,
those who will listen
and those who will value your life.

Canopy

The golden hymns of worship
bring in the new year.
Cross legged we sit
immersed in the message
of God and good,
eyes closed in spiritual comfort
helped by a lack of sleep
and a hangover,
greed and evil
mixed in
with sorrow and hope and gratitude
for life's benediction.

Intentions

I see your lips, red,
cheeks pinched
sucking on a straw
clogged with chocolate shake
as thick as freshly made concrete.
Black nails and black dress
crying out an indifference
to all but yourself,
your creamy cleavage
taunting and remote,
your dark eyes, piercing,
looking for an answer
I cannot give.
Your long eyelashes,
mesmerizing.
The proud burger
dies from neglect,
the fries secure
in their latticework
hold the copious layers of ketchup.

My knee touches yours,
you do not flinch or move,
your silence is not awkward,
my intention is.

We leave,
fries untouched.

Torment

Let the sun scorch my skin
So it feels cool
After your touch.
Let the snowfall
be heavy and silent
as it drifts onto
my upturned face
so I can focus on your essence
deep within me.
Let the monsoon rains
drench the land
and bring the fresh damp smell
of steaming earth
to my nostrils
as I walk barefoot
in my sodden and dripping clothes.
Darkness in the day
thunder and lightning
all bringing together
the vision
of your dark hair and eyelashes,
your lithe and sinuous form
exposed by your brilliant smile,
all sound now drowned
by the beating of my heart.

I stand on the mountain,
the wind whipping
my clothes, my hair, my skin
my eyes.
Cleansing tears flow freely,
your memory lifts me higher,
beyond the summit.
I cannot escape your presence
I cannot escape you.
Let me come home
into your arms, your heart,
your being.
Torment me no more.

I suck the salt

I suck the salt,
my tongue plays with the ice,
my head tilts far back
as the last drops of the margarita
trickle down my throat.
My eyes close
against the dim light
and the cacophony of sound
from a hundred mouths
as the image of your breast
brands my drunken eyelid.

The page (writer's block)

So quiet. So passive.

So imploring. So patient.

So inert.

The past, the future,

the present

linger and hover

in the particles of dirt,

so fine, unseen,

burdened by the weight they carry,

tired and apologetic

they settle

in a deepening embrace,

in empathy

with the inertia

of mind and of body.

The warm and lingering kiss

of the setting sun,

the sharp, golden rays fade away

into the lonely night.

Much before dawn,

a brilliant light,

unhurried movement,

a human breath

blows away

the cover of time,

the pages dissolve

with uninterrupted enthusiasm

of the inspired word,

pen and paper in harmony,

no consideration

of moving hands on the clock.

A new day dawns.

Shining shoals

My thoughts are as deep
as the ocean in front of me,
maybe not as dark,
maybe not as deep,
tingling,
teeming life with shiny reflections
near the surface,
in schools and in shoals
mitigates the inviting darkness
of inhospitable environs
as my thoughts hurriedly
return to sun and surf and sand
where smiles are more favored
than frowns,
even a desultory embrace
more welcome
than no touch at all.
Heels leave the frothing foam,
the tide runs out
as the sun sets
and steps lead me
to my own waiting darkness,
waiting for shiny shoals
to surface.

I will.
(Revolution)

Turn the wheels
hunch your back
turn them faster
take up the slack.
Muscles burn
as I take my turn,
tighten my grip,
sweat makes it slick,
men wait in line
all in their prime
to prove their strength
to prove their faith
for the same cause
to make it run
without a pause.
The world would know
that we were here
the world would know
there was no fear.
Together,
in all kinds of weather,
they would persevere
to shine a light
into the night,

to clear the mist
they would persist,
for nothing good came
without an 'I should',
to rid the world of ill
no truer words than
'I will'.

Tivas in the tide

The shimmering waves, silver
in the expanse of blue,
seaweed, sand and surf,
beer and vodka
chips and salsa,
waiters in black
of different hues.
Tivas in the tide
children on the slide,
lovers hand in hand,
the setting sun,
hesitant steps,
toes wiggling
in the trickling sand.
A lingering kiss,
a happy smile
tinged with sadness
that will last a while,
unable to share or write or send
a message to a friend.

The mirror

I look in the mirror
and see not my image
but the shell of memories
stretching into the moment
of my birth
for that is where it begins
showing,
how very finite I am.
I bounce back into my reflection
and cannot see my future.
I marvel at my mind
as it catches me in the present.
I look ahead
and see my finite end.
I hastily return to a life
that speedily moves
toward oblivion.

Blood

I have dripped away
from your heart,
thoughts written with a pen
that happens to be red.
Bright red emotions
congeal into dark thoughts
at your feet.
You walk away
leaving fading footprints
of red
on the cold concrete floor.

Anguish

I hold your hand in desperation
as I watch and feel you slip away,
the memory of cold fingers and warm heart
bittersweet.
The floor slips away
leaving me weightless,
suspended,
rudderless,
I keel over.
You have gone,
waiting for the flames
to consume you
and I wait
cold as ice,
looking at the darkness
over the horizon.
Will the sun ever shine again,
will a warm breeze
break the icicles
of fear and loneliness.
Will I ever feel complete.
You come to me in my dreams
to calm my restless cries
muffled by the pillow,

crushed within my fetal form.
Only time will deliver me
from this anguish
and this emptiness.

The asphalt road

The narrow asphalt road
pitted, convex, dignified
by a dusty gravel border
flowing into fields of saffron.
The mighty fort,
dusty,
merging with the steep walls
of rising earth,
defending nothing
yet,
defiant
for, it holds the
secrets of the intrigues
the losses, the defeats
the victories
of ambitious men
and indifferent women.
The lazy creaking of the wooden cart
silent on its rubber wheels,
still
disturbs the partridge
which whirs into shallow flight

and gains sanctuary
in the saffron field,
its dusty plumage
merging in its natural habitat.

I leave my love

I leave my love
wrapped up in flowers
on your grave,
they too will bloom
wither and die
but my love for you lives on,
an undefined ache
in my consciousness
that brings on a sigh, a smile,
a frown,
a shake of the head
but is closer to me
than my shadow,
for,
at night it looms large
in my loneliness
searching for relief
in the nooks and crannies
of my heart.
I find a memory,
I ask the unanswerable question,
Why?
Restless
I crumple the sheets
and speak a language of reconciliation.

Live with me and my love,
in companionship,
so I can smile again,
not forgetting you
for I cherish each moment
we had together.

A voice

A voice on the telephone
brings in my childhood.
A strong voice,
to comfort or scold,
to encourage or cajole
over passing years
time and tears
and increasing fears.
The voice on the telephone
now breathless,
occasionally forgetful
enquiring of mundane things,
telescoping my life
in a kaleidoscope
of emotions.

Perfection

I walk in the harsh glare of your presence.

Sometime, a little shade is welcome.

I breathe in your essence,

constantly.

Sometimes, a weary sigh escapes.

I look up at you

high on a pedestal

that I have built

and wish I can be your equal.

The path that I follow

will be my own,

the mistakes I make

I will own.

Will you judge me, correct me, help me,

guide me

or will I be in your blind spot

recognition never fulfilled.

Centuries disappear

Centuries disappear
in the void of time
so filled with hate
so filled with crime.
Scribes and tongues
hold thoughts and deed
to fill the emptiness
of lives we lead.
The past has already
whipped away
in a mighty slipstream
with irrevocable consequence,
the future receding
just as fast
always out of reach
of searching minds
and eager hands.
Only left
in its most transient form —
the Present.

Wash away

I ran into the waves.
Cold
water washes over me
indifferent to my need
for distraction
to think away
the presence of my past,
to wash away
sorrow and regrets
for a new beginning
probably, too late already,
each experience
tinged with suspicion,
cynical.
The loss of material life
held together
with a passing optimism,
'fill this nebulous void',
my only thought
as wave after wave
crashes from outside
and within,
to shake the burden
of thoughtful uncertainty,
as toes grip the sand

gain traction
into the present.
Salt water drips away.
It would be sacrilege
to wipe even one drop.

Patients – the list

Six foot two,

two eighty pounds.

Incision. Deep,

tight tissue.

Release, release, release.

Reconstruct.

Diseased tissue out,

Metal and plastic in.

Blood loss significant.

Replace, replace, replace.

Weary muscles. Mine.

A quick sandwich.

Rehydrated.

New patient.

Start on the shoulder.

Torn. Pain.

Weary muscles. His.

Home.

The big spine tomorrow.

My lady fair.

Woe to thee

my lady fair

for humble me

thou hast not a care.

My love blossoms

When'evr our eyes do meet

smitten as I am

with your smile so sweet.

The California Mall.

A stud in the nose
one in the ear,
profile hidden
by raven black hair.
Scarlet nails
holding a pen
with a chewed up end.
She rubs her Robin Hood shoe
against the black jeaned leg
of the spiky haired boy
teaching her retail tricks
of selling mobile phones
to overly made up teens
with bright eyes
and tight jeans
and perky breasts.
The little mobile booth
dwarfed
by the latte, cake and cookie stall.
See and be seen
in this cool, colored, controlled
fluorescent lit, sterile,
humming world
of buy and sell.
A very young, pregnant woman

licks her ice cream

in an anti-nausea fervor.

Her solicitous

even younger friend

carrying multiple bags,

brand names all.

Gaudy, glass fronted

doors, of shops

selling beyond useless stuff

to passionate people

of uncertain means.

The mostly purposeful strides

of the fashionable few,

co-mingled

with the luxurious strides

of the committed window shopper,

at odds

with the lack of human forms

outside

all hidden

in the ubiquitous motor vehicle.

An evening out

Surrounded by sound
immersed in the noise
contributing and competing
with each added decibel.
Drunk
in love,
in anticipation,
in celebration,
momentarily removed from
expectations to perform
at work,
at play,
at love.
Rejoice,
return to reality
and occasionally
drowning
in regret and recrimination,
foolish for companionship
and greater foolishness
to impress.
Pay the bill.
Bathe in the aura

of inebriation,

not necessarily alcoholic.

See what tomorrow brings.

Did today change anything?

Misty darkness

With a wink
and a touch
and a slither and a smile,
thigh to thigh,
leather against silk,
misty darkness
and the thunder of drums.
Unheard voices
with mistaken intent
and misleading smiles
blinking blue with the straub.
Nails and martinis,
brushing the sugar on the rim.
Spirits uplifted,
lips against ears,
fingers touch silken hair
with the thunder of drums.
Interlude in the powder room,
uncertainty
with the walk across the dance floor,
glitter shining on pale cheeks.
Darkness and light
reflecting

fluttering feelings.
The comforting, confident,
indulgent smile
clinches the night.

Justice

An ornate room
holding history
within its walls,
its subdued elegance
revealing stark truths,
uncovering lies
day after day.
Judgment comes in the form
of a black robe
and contained within,
grace and tact.
Rigidity
in the interpretation
of man made laws,
trying to avoid
a miscarriage of
justice.

A sleepy breath

Her head rested on my shoulder

gently

with comfort and love.

Each sleepy breath

took her deeper

into

what I can only hope

would be

dreams of happiness and fulfillment

that only

innocence can bring.

The journey

Each mile of life's journey
that I have travelled
in your presence
gave me the meaning of grace
and giving and living,
holding onto memories
of togetherness and laughter
that span the generations,
your generosity
enriching lives,
memories that
serve us so well.
We continue that journey
with a smile.

The Hospital Lobby

I lean against
the vending machine.
Cold, bright colors
offer me solace.
An inert mass
holding bubbles and cheer
in carbonated drinks
and caloric exuberance.
A button pressed
and remote levers travel
their carefully engineered paths
to deliver the goods
with a rumble and a clunk
but only for a price
reinforcing the age old lesson,
all things come at a price
which sometimes
we cannot pay
held back
by unbreakable
emotional chains.
My peripheral vision
takes in the diffuse
phosphorescent light
of the hospital lobby

as it bravely pushes

away the darkness

in one's life

and in one's soul.

Time ticking by in a vacuum

in silence

in hope

in despair,

unending.

Negotiate with me lord,

give me peace,

give me strength.

I will pay any price

though I really have nothing to give.

Time is ticking by,

I really do not have

anything to give.

My empty heart

As you lie on me
your lips
inches away from mine,
the comfort of your weight,
all skin,
drives away my fears
of being alone.
My empty heart
fills with love,
a pulsating force
carrying with it
the essential rhythm of life.
My arms
want to crush you
instead
my fingers play
a caressing game
on your back.
Your searching eyes
look into my soul.
Will you be mine
and I yours
for all eternity?
Say yes, say yes,
Say yes my love.

Silent tears

The gentle breeze
touches my bare shoulder,
intermittently,
produced by the rickety old fan
in the humid
otherwise silent night
but for the crashing surf
muted by the distance.
Tumultuous thoughts
elbow each other
to the forefront of consciousness
threaten to pry open
eyelids that are closed
to welcome sleep
that does not come.
My mind crawls out of cloying
negativity
into the reality of darkness
crying silent tears
of defeat.

Sadness

You have gone so far away from me.

Will I ever get you back.

A little tear of sadness

trickles out of my eye

every night

till sleep comes

to the rescue

but only till

the blossoming dawn,

with no escape

in the brilliant light of

each passing day.

There is a silent sadness

that creeps around inside

hidden from all

who will not see.

The Breeze

The cool currents of the breeze
flow around me
caress and wrap around me
to lift the mass of skin and bone
which does not budge.
Weary is the body
stuck to dirt and stone.
The eyes wander
over hill and dale,
take in the orange and purple sky.
the warmth of the day is gone,
the chill of the night
is creeping in.
The breeze continues to
dance its intimate dance
licking away the moisture
as every pore weeps
with joy that life,
sometimes brings.

Verbal bullets

The violence of your words
hits me like a hurricane
suddenly appearing
over a calm horizon.
My windows are not shuttered.
I am not prepared.
My vulnerable façade
is ripped away
leaving the inside
stinging with each speeding raindrop
or
is it the burning of tears
that escape like a scream
that nobody hears.

The soap bubble.

Froth and soap and bubbles
arising from a cheery warmth
of enveloping water.
The perfect orb
of translucent surfactant
breaks away
rises and floats
catching the light
and many colors
happy in its freedom
and the joy it brings
to watching eyes.
A painted fingernail
lazily comes from the water
touches the frolicking bubble.
A brief life
a glorious death.

Some poems from the first book-
Invisible Hands, a book of poetry.

Last night

The golden rays of
the early morning sun
touch her hair.
Her gentle breathing
muffled
by the rumpled sheets
that cover her carelessly,
the painted toe nail
peeking out,
as her foot
dangles off the edge.
I remember her delight,
last night
at retrieving the sprinkled cup cake
from the little brown bag
and wolfing it down
with the chilled champagne
as she looked at me
so directly
so invitingly,
last night.

Surgery

Hands move

in controlled ecstasy,

immersed

in nature's beauty gone wrong.

The depths are exposed

illuminated by artificial light

and the wisdom of years.

The dance of the fingers

choreographed by experience,

synchronous

with the aim

of initiating

a cure

of a malady

inflicting

this unfortunate body.

My daughter

I have looked upon
and adored this face
for all these years.
The addition of her life,
her energy, her laugh,
her silences to mine
has forever
completed the purpose
of my existence.
Every moment of togetherness
shared
is a ray of sunshine
to a starving soul.
It is the quantum of strength
that builds the core,
to overcome
most of what
life throws at me.

The gentle waltz

The woman tripped along
her heart full of song,
a lazy smile on her lips
and a graceful
wiggle to her hips.
Golden light bathed
the countryside,
vanishing dew drops
glittered before they died.
She saw the welcoming meadow
with the white wooden gate,
she hurried through it,
a trifle late.
He lay amongst the flowers
waiting for her,
blue eyes drinking blue sky,
fingers flitting over the petals,
fingers stroking the stems.
He sensed her presence
and rose
like life itself
from Mother earth.
She ran into the arms
of her beau,
crushed in his embrace,

declaration of love
coming at a fevered pace,
her body arching to his,
fingertips wandering
to undo her lace.
Spent,
they drifted above
in a gentle waltz,
their bodies entwined
in a cocoon of love.

www.ingramcontent.com/pod-product-compliance
Lightning Source LLC
LaVergne TN
LVHW021359080426
835508LV00020B/2355